Maureen's insights have powerful paybacks. She not only knows how women succeed; she equips you to do it for yourself.

--Debra Benton, author *The CEO Difference: How to Climb, Crawl, and Leap Your Way to the Next Level of Your Career*

This series helps women to discover the most important truth in advancing their leadership: You are the most powerful change agent in your own journey. A must read for anyone committed to unleashing the ingenuity and talent of half our population in order to create innovative solutions for *all* of us.
--Tiffany Dufu, Chief Learning Officer, Levo League

Do you want to talk about growth or do you want to grow? If you want to grow, start here. Accessible and practical, Maureen Berkner Boyt's books give you advice that will propel you straight out of your comfort zone into a whole new world. Just do it!
--Jodi Detjen, Suffolk University Professor and co-author, *The Orange Line: A Woman's Guide to Integrating Career, Family and Life*

Make no mistake—mentors do matter. When you need real world advice to gain and retain your seat at the leadership table, look no further. This highly readable

book series stands in as your personal sponsor, showing you actionable steps and providing that pat on the back and gentle shove forward we all need from time to time. So, *Rock Your Moxie* --take action, take risk, and take charge.
--Connie Duckworth, Founder/CEO, ARZU STUDIO HOPE and author of *The Old Girls' Network: Insider Advice to Women Building Businesses in a Man's World*

Finally a book series for women that connects all the dots! Whether you're a senior executive or emerging leader, Maureen's Power Moves will get you in winning shape and stretching beyond boundaries.
--Linda Bernier, Senior Vice President, Trizetto Corporation

Maureen's core message—"Get off your tush and do it!"-- is energizing and her moxie is contagious. Readers will inhale the books and race to start implementing Maureen's sensible and concrete leadership advice.
--Meg Cadoux Hirshberg, author, *For Better or For Work: A Survival Guide for Entrepreneurs and Their Families*

Maureen Berkner Boyt is refreshingly candid, insightful, and even a bit edgy as she delivers real world advice and strategies all women can use. Made for any woman

wanting to achieve more or be more, this series is a guidebook for making it happen.
--Alison Martin-Books, CEO of Mentoring Women's Network, Author of *"Landing on My Feet: Learning to Lead Through Mentoring"*

Maureen Berkner Boyt has a winner here for women who are focused on succeeding in big ways - for themselves, their companies, communities and the world. Her *Rock Your Moxie* series enables women to take their place at any table - business, government, world tables - at a time when women's voices are so sorely needed.
--Barbara Osterman, Founder and President, Human Solutions LLC

Maureen Berkner Boyt is a high performance leader who shares her top notch formula for women to win in the new world of work. In her Rock Your Moxie series, she focuses on straight talk and best practices that elevate effectiveness that takes women to the next level. Whether you're on the corporate ladder or building your own business, the insights and information in this series is relevant, actionable and just what women leaders need to hear right now.
--Lisa Hendrickson, President, Spark City

Maureen Berkner Boyt has put together a series of invaluable knowledge and insights that help women rise to their potential and harness their strengths. Maureen's books on leadership are an invaluable resource and must have in this ever changing, hyper speed world. I will be keeping mine at arms reach on my desk so that I can refer to them daily.
--Tamara Kleinberg, serial entrepreneur & founder of TheShuuk.com

Rock Your Moxie is for women leaders who are already committed to playing big. If this isn't your first rodeo and you're looking for a way to seriously step up your game, then you just picked up a game changer. In this series, Maureen Berkner Boyt brilliantly provides chapter after chapter of meaningful clarity and guidance garnered from lessons learned in the trenches. Full of breakthrough takeaways and tangible tools, be prepared to rock your world.
--Kris Boesch, Founder & CEO, Choose People

Rock Your Moxie: Power Moves for Women Leading the Way

5 Strategies for Warp Speed Growth

Maureen Berkner Boyt

5 *Strategies for Warp Speed Growth.* Copyright © 2012 by Maureen Berkner Boyt. All rights reserved. No part of this book may be reproduced or used without written permission. For information and permissions, contact Reiden Publishing, 1112 Oakridge Dr.#104-265 Fort Collins, CO 80525.

Copyright ©2012 Reiden Publishing

This series is dedicated to my tribe, the women of the world who are committed to growth, leading the way and making a difference.

Keep rocking your moxie!

Table of Contents

Preface 1

Chapter 1: Live On The Skinny Branches 9

    Chapter 1 Power Moves 16

Chapter 2: Suck It Up And Shake It Off 19

    Chapter 2 Power Moves 25

Chapter 3: Pay To Play 28

    Chapter 3 Power Moves 32

Chapter 4: Get Your Happy On 35

    Chapter 4 Power Moves 41

Chapter 5: Ask Until Your Knees Shake 43

    Chapter 5 Power Moves 49

Conclusion: Pulling It All Together 52

The 25 Power Moves 54

Author Biography 63

Preface

You are not alone. You picked up this book because you are a successful woman who wants *more*. You are want to be more, have a bigger impact, make more money, and call bigger and bigger shots. I wrote this series to help you accelerate that process and to help catapult you forward from wherever you are today. Success and leadership are not rocket science, but they require thinking the right way and doing the right things, consistently.

I've done the research for you. I've spent the past few years interviewing some of the brightest, most dynamic, successful women in the business world. I've also traveled the country visiting local chapters of The Moxie Exchange Movement and engaging in meaningful business and leadership conversations with professional women who are investing in their own learning and growth. I've spent hundreds of hours around rock star female leaders discussing and dissecting leadership and success for women. I've paid attention, watched for patterns, taken notes, and distilled the ideas here – for you. I'm sharing what I've learned in this book and in the *Rock Your Moxie* series.

Each book covers five ideas with five coinciding Power Moves that will propel you forward. The books are designed to be short, powerful and pack a punch. Think of reading them as being akin to participating in a full-body contact sport rather than being a spectator at that same game. Growing personally and as a leader is work. It requires that you get off the sidelines, take off your protective gear, and get in there and play to your full potential. I know you are up to the challenge. I suggest you read a chapter at a time, digest the information, and take action on the ideas that really resonate with you.

I'll refer to the knowing/doing gap throughout the books. That's the place where average performers live. It's the gap between saying, 'Well of *course* I should do that. Everybody knows *that*.' to actually getting off your tush and doing it. Crossing the gap means making the changes and implementing the ideas and thinking that high performing women use everyday. Be thinking about how the ideas apply to you, be honest in your assessment of where you stand and move forward toward being a better leader and more successful version of who you are today.

I want you to succeed in a ridiculously big way. I want that for you individually and for us collectively as women. So, I don't pull any punches and I'm not blowing smoke up anyone's skirt in the books. There are bigger issues at play here. It's time to change the face of leadership in the business world. This last decade was supposed to be the time when women made gains that brought us close to parity in the boardroom and executive suite, and instead the needle has barely moved. That gets me wrapped around the axle. Why? Long ago power was held in the church, more in recently government and now it rests in the business world. If we're going to make a positive difference in the world, we need women at the table.

We need YOU at the table.

If you really want to make the abysmal stats about male/female ratios in leadership positions come to life, spend some time on the 'Executive Team' and 'Leadership Team' pages of mid to large sized companies. If you're prone to high blood pressure, I don't recommend this activity for you. It is truly appalling- page after page of middle-aged white guys in various colored ties and stages of male pattern baldness peppered by the occasional woman.

I swear I've gone through four of the five stages of grief in this process: denial, anger, bargaining, and depression. But, HELL NO, I am not landing on the last stage of 'acceptance'!

Let me be clear that I have nothing against middle-aged white guys. I'm married to a spectacular one, we need men in leadership positions, and this isn't about 'us vs. them' and victimization. It is about how we move the dial on the numbers. It's about making the numbers 'real' for decision makers. It's about stepping up and owning your own abilities and throwing your name in the hat when opportunities arise. It's about finding mentors and sponsors to propel your career, and being the same to women coming up behind you. Whatever you do, don't 'accept' that this is the way things have been and will always be in the business world.

When things are terrible, people get fired up and start making changes. When things are 'good enough' complacency sets in. In the business world, things are 'good enough' for women right now. There are enough opportunities in middle management that the lack of women in the C-suite isn't causing an uproar. The days of butt-pinching machismo are for the most part a distant memory. In fact men and women are getting along just swimmingly, so the fact that women are only making 77% of what men earn is barely causing a yawn. Women no longer have to bring their husbands along to co-sign for a business loan (which was happening as recently as the late 80's) so the fact that they rarely have access to the big money (1 million-plus loans, venture and angel dollars) doesn't cause a stir.

Things are just good enough that they are killing us in terms of forward progress. The dial on critical factors (pay, executive positions, board of directors' seats, elected office…) has barely moved in the past 15 years. It's a sad state of affairs. And guess what? It impacts YOU.

What to do? Step up, step out and move the dial. If things are going to change collectively, as women we need to grow individually. That starts with you committing to your own growth as you read this book. That takes me back to wanting you to be ridiculously successful for you and for "us".

On the issue and impact of the dearth of women leaders in business, we've got to change the numbers, and that means taking action. Roll up your sleeves, and create a plan as you read. Really use the Power Moves section at the end of each chapter to help guide your planning and ensuing action. By the end of the series you should have a rock-solid, kick butt, get-after-it plan for success and owning your place at the next summit in your leadership journey. I look forward to hearing your stories of success, leadership and how you're getting after it in a big way! Send me an *email mo@moxieexchange.com* or join the conversation and community tribe on my blog *www.moxieexchange.com/blog* Rock your moxie!

Maureen Berkner Boyt

Javea, Spain / Fort Collins, Colorado

Chapter 1:

Live On the Skinny Branches

When is the last time that you've done something that really made you feel alive? That you thought to yourself, 'I can't believe I'm actually doing this!' while in the moment. Something that took your breath away in its audacity. When? Have you been heeding Eleanor Roosevelt's advice to "Do one thing every day that scares you."?

As far as I know, complete strangers in Japan, Germany and the US have naked photos of me. A few weeks back, in the pouring rain, I stripped down and jumped off a small cliff into the Fairy Pools on the Isle of Skye with the small knot of bystanders, who materialized when I started shedding clothes, snapping photos. I knew the water would be so cold it would literally take my breath away (at 6C/43F it did), that I would need to get naked in front of strangers (I did) and that I would have to face one of my big fears (heights) to take the plunge.

Not only did I jump, I got out, scrambled back up the rocks and cliff and jumped AGAIN for good measure. Hell yeah, sister. I was ALIVE! I leapt for the sheer wild joy of it. I jumped so my kids could see me face a fear and do it anyway. I jumped to prove to myself that I could, and that, as I said to my husband with a wink when we walked off down the path after my jumps, "I've still got it." Twenty years ago I took a similar plunge into the Colorado River and I needed to prove to myself that although I am more responsible these days, I am just as fearless.

I took the plunge because I knew if I didn't I would always think to myself, "I should have." Those folks with the photos of me have photos. I have the experience and visceral reminder that the good stuff in life, those big experiences, aren't going to happen unless you're willing to take the plunge. One of the Germans with a camera, a guy of about 25 said, "You are crazy, girl!", as I was heading back for round 2. You're damned straight I am, Skippy! I am crazy - full of life, ideas, action and forward momentum. I am willing to do something that scares me to get the big rewards. That's the key.

If you want to grow fast, it's not going to happen if you're playing it safe.

A key strategy for kicking it into high gear is getting out there on what I call *the skinny branches*. You know the place I'm talking about. The high risk, high reward, I've-never-been-here-before domain. For those willing to go there, it's really an extraordinary place to learn and grow as a leader and a person. It's a place high performers seek out and spend a LOT of time in.

To get out on skinny branches you have to face failure and fear, so most people stay in the safe, slow-growth zone. That 1-2 punch is too much for them to stomach. An even bigger nut to crack can be getting over your fear OF failure. Leaders, though, have totally different paradigms for fear and failure. They understand that high performance involves being comfortable with taking risk and failing *into* success. They get it that failure is a part of the growth and success equation. Nobody gets it right every, single time unless they are doing exactly the same things in exactly the same ways that they always have. That's a pattern of stagnation. It's very predictable, and will get you exactly nowhere. Think of failure instead as an accelerator, rather than as something you spend energy trying to avoid. It's simply an expected part of the process of growth and if you're not failing, it's an indication that you're not growing.

If you want fast growth, you also have to be willing to move through fear. Amelia Earhart said it beautifully, "Our fears are paper tigers." The majority of our fears are self-imposed. They exist only between our own ears. The fact of the matter is we manufacture every fear we have except that of loud noises and falling, which we are born with. Research has found that we can pretty quickly pick up 'evolutionary fears' of things that really can potentially harm us (snakes, spiders, heights, water) because those fears can serve to protect us. Other than that, it's all you, baby. Here's the beautiful thing about getting those manufactured fears under control; they hate the light of day. Fears have their tightest grip on us when we continue to spin them in our own minds. So don't. Talk about them with someone. Name them. Get clear on what's behind your fear. Once you name a fear and bring it out for review, the power that fear exerts decreases exponentially.

Slightly over 6 months after The Moxie Exchange Movement launched, we held our first mentoring event for teenaged girls, MoxieFest. That put me WAY out on the skinny branches. We took a risk- we didn't have the time or the money to pull it off, and we still went for it because it was in alignment with our values and what's important to us. Holding the event so quickly was a reminder that the timing will NEVER be right, and that we have to do things that make us uncomfortable. I had all sorts of between-the-ears fears about why we shouldn't hold MoxieFest, but when I really dug in and looked at them, I understood that they were all self-imposed. They were 'trunk clinging' thoughts and a great example of the limits we tend to set for ourselves that serve to slow our growth. Sure, there were little screw-ups during that first event but we used those small failures from year one to make year two of the event even more powerful.

Here's one more strategy for living on the skinny branches, failing forward and slaying your fears: don't forget to laugh. I've made some epic dives from the skinny branches. I'm talking crash and burn stupid moves. I've taken a page from my teenaged son Caiden's book on this one. He likes to MUni (mountain-unicycle). Yup, you read that right; he rides steep, gnarly mountain trails on one wheel. When he goes down, he goes down *hard*. When he comes up, he's bleeding AND laughing at the same time, usually with a "Did you SEE that?" whoop of joy. If you're going to dig it, enjoy the crash, because if you spend too much time licking your wounds or beating yourself up, you won't get out there again anytime soon. When Cade goes down, he doesn't give up, head home, and shove his MUni in the garage because he fell. He doesn't sit in the trail and berate himself for wiping out. He doesn't take the easier choice in routes after he bites it. He makes sure someone *saw* his crash, he laughs, he figures out why he crashed and then he hops back on and heads back up the trail.

The hell with fear, then! To hell with seeing failure as terminal! Kick those thoughts to the curb and press on. Get out there on the skinny branches. Do something TODAY to feel alive and strong conquer your fears. Climb out there on the skinny branches and stretch yourself and watch your growth start to soar!

Chapter 1 Power Moves

1. Pick a decision you've found yourself holding back on and playing it safe about, and create a 'worst case scenario' chart to help you move forward. At the top, write down the decision, with three columns below it. In column 1, write down the worst case scenario, in column 2, how

you'll know you've gotten there/indicators you have reached the worst case, in column 3 what action you will take.

2. Host a lunch/happy hour in honor of your biggest screw up. Own, celebrate, laugh, and discuss when things didn't go as planned. Share what you learned and how the 'failure' has helped move you forward.

3. Name your fears and talk them down. "If I do "x" I'm afraid that "y" will happen."

4. Do a debrief on the things you're initially categorizing as a 'failure'. Answer these questions: What went right? What did I learn? How did I just fail forward toward success?

5. Have a fan club. Yes, a fan club. Have a few key people from your inner circle that you have set up an explicit arrangement with

in advance so they understand their role. When you are feeling fearful or worried about failing, call them up or meet with them to say, "This is scaring the crap out of me!" or, "I'm about to go really, really big on this one." Their job is to tell you that you are a brilliant rock star, you've got this, and that they are holding the safety net for you. They are not there to go through contingency plans, or cost benefit analysis. They are there to push your butt out on the skinny branch and cheer you on. Trust me, it works.

Chapter 2:

Suck It Up and Shake It Off

What awaits you when you walk into a Paralympic swim meet? Prosthetic legs strewn about the pool deck. Guide dogs. Empty wheelchairs. And elite athletes in action making it all look easy. The sheer athleticism of the group is an incredible sight to see. What you won't find, and what I've never heard, are excuses or whining. No complaining that things are too hard, that something hurts, that they should be given a break. Trust me; this group would have every right to do that and more. Many of them live with daily pain. All of them live with some form of physical disability ranging from almost full paralysis, to missing limbs to blindness. Yet there's not a whiner to be found in the group.

Life can be hard. Leadership *is* hard. Sometimes we have to do things we simply don't like or be in situations we would rather take a pass on. Life can serve up some truly crappy circumstances. How should we handle it? As my good friend Sara once told me, *"Suck it up, cupcake!"*

I've been known to whine occasionally in my life. Actually, my brother and sisters used to call me "Screamin' " when I was little because I would scream until I fainted when I was angry or things weren't going my way. (Cut me a little slack- I stopped that charming practice when I was 3, but the nicknamed endured.) As for early in my career, what did complaining get me? It certainly didn't win me any points with co-workers, and it didn't improve my mindset any.

My internal dialogue of 'that's not fair' or 'this is hard' only served as a governor on my ability to lead and succeed. It was, and remains, a losing practice.

If you want to grow fast, leave the bitching, complaining, excuses and whining in the dust.

When I feel the urge to complain, I ask myself a series of questions to get my attitude and mindset pointed forward and up. 'This is hard compared to *what*?' 'Is anyone going to die?' 'Am I going to learn something from the challenge?' Every time I end up with the same conclusion- time to suck it up, learn a lesson, if there is one and move on. Nobody wants to hear your drama or woes. Really. They don't. If you feel obliged to share, you're shooting yourself in the success, career and business foot. Knock it off. Think about the most successful women you know. How much time to they spend complaining about their challenges or circumstances? I'll throw down for another bottle of Spanish wine and wager that your answer will be very, very little to none. They are focused forward, not spending energy on complaining and excuses.

    My daughter had a swim race recently that can only be described as ugly. Her technique was terrible and her time was slower than anything she'd raced in years. It was a bit painful to watch. It was also very public, with her name and race time up on the scoreboard for all to see. Oh, and she was almost naked at the time as race suits these days seem to consist of about 4 square inches of fabric. So, we had a 15- year old, mostly naked girl failing in public, which would seem to add up to a recipe for a very big meltdown. Not so. I knew she was going to be just fine because she has an incredible ability to shake things off. It's almost astonishing how fully she leaves it all in the pool, bad or good.

I love watching her at the end of a race. She touches the wall and immediately looks up at the clock. Either a wide grin spreads across her face or she gives a small headshake, depending on what the numbers read. Then she hops out of the pool, shakes herself off, and heads over to cool down and talk with her coaches. When the race is done, it's done. She takes it in, debriefs on what worked and what didn't, and moves on. She doesn't beat herself up or replay the tape again and again in her head when a race goes bad. When it goes well, she enjoys the moment. She's got the mental toughness that it takes to succeed in sports.

At 16, she's mastered what it has taken me years to learn. Failures, a mistake, a bad call in business or leadership are all things to learn from, shake off and move beyond. Sara Blakely of Spanx attributes failure as one of her top success tools. In the last chapter I talked about failing forward. Here's the other half the equation; it's not just our ability to fail but also *our ability to fail PLUS the ability to quickly shake it off and move on that accelerates our success.*

I spent years failing, and then beating the hell out of myself mentally for the failures. Yes, I had learned from the failures and was farther along, but somehow I had missed the part about letting it go, too. I could have won a gold medal in mental self-flagellation. I wasted a lot of mental energy replaying tapes in my head of my failures and mistakes.

Watching my daughter shake it off after a bad race has been an eye-opener for me. She fails, she learns, she moves on. All the learning, none of the guilt. It's a beautiful thing. When I start down the mental-replay-punching-bag path, I pull up an image of my daughter at the end of a bad race looking up, hopping out of the pool, and shaking it off. Then I shake it off and move forward, too.

Beware of rolling around in your successes for too long, too. It's an equally dangerous practice. We all know people who bring up awards they've won or triumphs they've had in the past. Heck yeah I want to celebrate my wins and the wins of others, but not past their expiration date. Watching my daughter shake it off after a great race has been as eye opening as watching her after a bad race. Fist pump, smile, cool down, debrief, time to move on and get focused on the next race. If you're focused on the past, whether good or bad, you're taking your eye off forward momentum and progress.

Chapter 2 Power Moves

1. Take all your gripes, complaints, slights, bad blood, excuses, health issues etc and write them on individual slips of paper. Really purge. Get it all out. Place them in a

fireplace or fireproof container (old coffee cans work great), light a match, drop it in, burn the hell out of them and ceremonially LET THEM GO. I've done this with everyone from highly successful executives to teenagers and every time it's pure magic.

2. Tune in to the conversations you are a part of. You're going to be amazed how much victim talk surrounds you. Make a vow to not chime in when excuses, blame, or complaints come up. Either change the conversation or walk away.

3. When you feel the urge to throw a pity party bubbling up, ask yourself these three questions: "This is hard compared to *what*? Is anyone going to die? What am I supposed to learn from this?"

4. When you find yourself replaying a failure, literally tell yourself, "Stop! We've moved on from that." Refocus by rewriting a goal you are working on. Determine two clear action items, that you can complete by the end of the day, toward accomplishing that goal.

5. Create visual prompts or mental cues to remind yourself to suck it up and shake it off. Photos, screen savers, and vivid memories that you can draw up quickly all work well.

Chapter 3:

Pay To Play

Women spend a *lot* of money on clothes, hair and coffee. The averages, for example, $50,000 on hair in a lifetime, are really staggering. We'll write big fat checks at the drop of the hat for our kids to play competitive sports, get music lessons, or have the latest gaming technology. We'll help a friend, or a complete stranger through charitable giving. But ask women to invest in our own learning and growth and suddenly things are WAY too expensive.

There are a multitude of reasons for this, depending on the woman. They range from fear of actually having to show up and make real change, fear of showing up and feeling inadequate, not understanding that if you don't learn and grow your career or business won't either, setting a 'deserving' level that is set really low, feeling guilty that investing time and money in her own growth is somehow selfish and so forth.

There is a real difference here between men and women. For men it's not whether they're going to invest in themselves, it's about "Where?" and "How much?" They're ready, willing, and able to spend money and time to move the dial for themselves, in many different ways. Case in point: men will drop thousands of dollars and hundreds of hours a year on golf. Golf. Why? Because they know that not only is it a good time, it's a good investment in their careers. They can connect the dots between the putting green and building relationships, getting the latest information on what's happening in the business community and sealing some deals. They unapologetically put themselves in as many learning and growth environments as they can, knowing that doing so equals increased exposure to people, ideas, tools and success. They will drop the money and invest the time for a seminar or a coach without batting an eye because they know it will help move them forward.

I've been polling organizational development leaders and executive coaches lately about this phenomenon, and to a person they see the same disparity. It's really, really troubling. If we want to see changes in the numbers at the top and in pay equity, we've GOT to be willing to invest time and money in building our own capabilities.

In more blunt terms, you've got to pay to play.

The super successful women in my life have this rapid-growth strategy down. One of the fundamental bedrocks of on-going success is actually having a strategy and plan in place for growth. One of my favorite women in the world started with very little in life and now owns two successful businesses and is an adjunct professor. She shared with me that she spends at least two days a quarter at a seminar or conference, and works on-going with an executive coach. She exemplifies fast-growth women. They budget the dollars, spend the time, and invest in learning. Why? Because they understand that if they want to make more money and be more successful, THEY need to grow. It doesn't happen in reverse order. You've got to grow your way into your success and the fastest way to do that is to make the commitment and investment. One of the greatest gifts we can give the people we love is our own development. As we become more, we can achieve more. We'll have bigger experience and ideas to share with them, and more financial resources to provide for them. The truly selfish act then is to choose NOT to invest in your own growth.

Because you're reading this book, I know you're at least part of the way there. You're interested in growing. You're on the success path. You want more. You're willing to invest in yourself, your relationships, and your development to some degree. My question to you is: are you all in? Are you nickel and diming yourself, or making a real investment? You've got to pay to play. I want you thinking like a guy right now. I want you knowing, feeling, and believing that an investment in your own growth is going ratchet up your success level in a big, big way. Game on.

Chapter 3 Power Moves

1. Add a 'learning and growth' line to your budget. You should be spending at least as much annually on your professional and

leadership learning and development as you are on your 'external' brand (clothes, shoes, hair, makeup, jewelry.) The money IS there. It's about making the choice on where you're going to spend it.

2. Subscribe to a few good magazines or blogs that are focused on leadership and success. You'll learn from their content and also find out about good programs and resources by what they are covering.

3. Poll successful women in your life about places they go for learning and growth. Ask them what organizations, programs and resources have contributed to their growth and success.

4. Commit 30 minutes a day to learning. Block it in your calendar.

5. Start a learning library. Start building up books, audios etc. that have been recommended to you as growth building blocks.

Chapter 4:

Get Your Happy On

Whenever I start to take myself too seriously, I wear pigtails. It's really hard to get stressed out or be a downer when you're sporting the hairstyle you wore when you were three. Trust me on this. I also reach out to women who fill me up and make me laugh. It always works. By making the choice to create an environment where I feel happy (pigtails) and surrounding myself with happy people (funny, smart girlfriends), my mood gets much lighter and I'm back on track.

We now know that when you're laughing, you're learning. We also know that who you hang around really impacts how you feel. Some smarty-pants researchers at Harvard and UC San Diego proved it, in case you were thinking this whole happiness thing is a load of crap. Go ahead and do your own little experiment if you like. Seek out and spend an hour with the happiest people you know and pay attention to how much better you feel after that hour. Their affect on you is a little like being sprinkled with happy dust.

A buckle-your-seatbelt growth strategy is to BE the happy person people seek out. You see, as Colin Powel said, "Perpetual optimism is a force multiplier." When you get your happy on, in a genuine way, possibilities seem endless. Your energy is up and the people around you get in the believing state of mind, too. Your joy creates an ecosystem around you of forward momentum, laughter and creativity.

Two of the most optimistic, genuine, friendly women I know are Kelli Tangney

Williams and Katy Piotrowski. I can recall for you *exactly* when I met both of these women, even though it's been almost 25 years since I met Kelli and 10 years since I met Katy. They both light up a room, and you want to be around them. You want to hear what they have to say. You want to drink whatever is in their Kool-Aid and see if you can get seconds, too. THAT is as powerful as it gets. Not surprisingly they are both very successful in their chosen paths, have strong relationships with their families and are respected and loved by the people in their lives. *Happiness is a strategy for success!*

Kelli and I were college roommates and occasionally she'd get what she called 'the Sunday night blues.' On those Sunday evenings she'd start to get quiet, and a little morose, that the weekend was over and it was back to class, homework and work in a few hours. It was like someone threw a dimmer switch on over our entire apartment. All of us were a little quieter.

All of us got glum. Holy influence, Batgirl! I learned from her that when you consistently bring your joy you elevate the people around you into feeling that way, too. Equally important was that if you're the person people are expecting happiness from, it can throw them off if you hit a glum patch. Luckily, I also learned that peanut butter and chocolate milk would perk Kelli right back up and get her back on track. She didn't need much, nor do any of us if we want to turn it around, to get back to optimistic and happy.

Think of ways you can amp up the joy in your business or department, too, because it turns out happy workplaces beat the pants off unhappy companies in profitability, retention, lost time and a host of other factors. Kris Boesch, Founder of Choose People, has the best blog out there on having happy employees. Her company completed 1,000 hours of research and they have the secret sauce (8 key factors) for creating an organization where people feel good about coming to work. I'll take fries with that secret sauce, please!

We've had a lot of people comment on the energy and happiness that surrounds The Moxie Exchange Movement. What a compliment! We really have set out to build an organization where you don't have to check your fun-factor at the door. We know we can drive business results faster and farther when we're in an atmosphere of joy. You can really be a 'serious' business organization or 'serious' about your career and leadership and still have fun. Life's too short to go to another boring business meeting, or be a part of a boring organization. Been there, done that, got the tee shirt. The person who best articulated what we're doing was Simone Marean, the Executive Director of the Girl's Leadership Institute. She looked at me and simply said, "There's strength in joy." Yes, yes, yes! That is it *exactly*. Choosing joy is choosing strength and choosing growth.

Seriously, this should not come as a shock. Think about when your best ideas came to you or the teams you were working with were really cranking it out. What bosses have you really given it your all for? What companies have you worked for that you really loved? When have you seen the people in your life really responding to you and helping you succeed, how were you showing up? The thread of optimism and happiness will be woven throughout those scenarios.

As always, it circles back to choice. How you're showing up, whom you're hanging out with, what you're doing as a company. Think about what you're doing in business and in life to create joy and growth for yourself and those around you. Remember that there's strength in joy.

I'll give you extra credit if you send me a picture of you in pigtails!

Chapter 4 Power Moves

1. Wake up every day and choose happiness and joy. If you get off track, remember that you can choose again. Create joy in your world.

2. Pick one thing to keep with you that is guaranteed to make you smile. I used to carry a small picture of my husband's high school graduation photo with me (he was wearing a blue velvet tux) and would pull it out when I needed a lift.

3. Get really interested in other people and tuned in to their emotions, especially the people closest to you. Figure out the things that you do consistently and authentically that make you and other people feel good. Do more of them.

4. Choose your news media carefully. Sensationalism and fear sell, so that's what the news is loaded with. Watching it has a big impact on your well- being. Consider skimming only headlines from a few different sources.

5. Build some silliness into your life. For example, on Friday mornings I hold what is known in our household as 'Friday morning dance party.' I turn on bad 80's music and shake my bootie all around the kitchen. My teenagers, who are wiped out by that point of the week truly *cannot* stop themselves from laughing, and I feel great, too.

Chapter 5:

Ask Until Your Knees Shake

Are you willing to leave 2 million dollars on the table? Because women ask for raises and promotions 85% less often than men, and when they do ask, it's for 35% less, so we're doing just that! Because women ask less, and ask *for* less, the financial implications over our careers are staggering. This doesn't just apply to money. We're asking for less and negotiating about less across the board. We don't ask for choice assignments, or lower interest rates, or more dollars to finance our businesses or travel upgrades. And we get what we ask for.

Linda Babcock and Sara Laschever have written two brilliant books on the topic that I highly recommend you read -- *Women Don't Ask* and *Ask For It.*. The first is more about the research and findings on women and negotiations; the second is more of a 'how to.' They found two key factors that contribute to women negotiating less and asking for less: *women don't realize what opportunities for negotiation exist and are worried about the social consequences of asking.*

My first job out of college was with an incredible company working for an extraordinary leader. There was an economic recession at the time, and college graduates were finding it hard to land jobs. I remember it like it was yesterday - my new boss offering me the position and telling me the salary, $18,000 annually. I felt *lucky* to have landed the job and *never even considered asking for more money*, even though I was making significantly more money per hour in my waitressing job. Fast forward a few months to a conversation with one of my male friends and co-workers who started at the same time and in the same role. He was making $24,000 a year. Why? Because he asked. I didn't, he did, and he got $6,000 more a year in his pocket.

Even after I found this out, I didn't ask for a raise because I didn't want to seem greedy, and I knew that the economy was rocky at the time. I was a classic case study for women and negotiations. I didn't know I could or should ask for more money in the first place, and even when I knew I should be making more, I was worried I would seem like a money-grubber. If only I knew then what I know now.

You have got to start asking for things at a level that seems ludicrous to you. You've got to ask until your knees shake. When you start to do this, and understand that asking is a key strategy for growth, prosperity and success, you will see all of those things skyrocket for you.

When you next have the opportunity to ask for a raise or negotiate a fee, get a number in your head. Now add 35%. You're probably just hitting the range that your male co-worker or competitor is asking for. What's the worst that can happen? If you are prepared, are 'likeable' in your negotiations (sadly the research shows this is key to our success in this regard) and state your case clearly, you are probably going to get very close to what you are asking for. Even if you hear a flat-out no, you are no worse off than you were before you asked! You are in the exact same place you were before you asked!

I painfully watched the male/female difference play out again recently with my own kids, who were about to start working for my husband. He asked them both how much they thought they should make per hour, and had them tell him independently what their salary requests were. My daughter: $8 per hour. My son: $12 per hour. When he asked their reasoning, our daughter shared that she was happy to have the job and that she didn't want to impact the cash flow of the business too much. Our son was all about how having him around would be a huge help to his dad and that he deserved at least that amount… and could he have a cut of profits, too? Classic female/male behavior.

My husband knew about the research, so went back to them for round two. He asked them again how much they thought they should make, asking if their first number was their final number. He even prompted my daughter to focus on the positive impact she would have on the business when coming up with her number. This time around my son asked for $100 an hour. Straight-faced. He had reasons, and a formula for why he really should make that much, and probably wouldn't take the job if he wasn't going to make that hourly rate. My daughter? $12.

I am not a shrinking violet and neither is my daughter. People have used phrases like 'force of nature' to describe both of us, yet we both sold ourselves short in a massive way. I share these personal examples because I believe that negotiations and asking for less is something that it's easy to intellectualize. You might be thinking, "Oh yes. I've heard about this." Here's my slap upside the head wake-up call for you:

You've been burned by this too. These statistics are about YOU.

You have got to own that this impacts you and commit to changing it for yourself. Our society has wired girls and women from a very young age not to ask and not to negotiate. There is good news, though. A good part of this battle is about understanding the issue and then about learning a new skill and implementing behavior changes.

It's also about recognizing our own biases that it's okay for men to ask, and not acceptable for women. Each of us needs to take a long, hard look in the mirror and see how we are contributing to the issue. Are you saying 'yes' to women as frequently as you are to men? Are you encouraging the women in your life to ask for more? Are you paying the women in your organization as much as the men? Giving them the same stretch opportunities? We didn't get to these stats in a vacuum. You need to start asking until your knees shake, and making it okay, even encouraging it for other women, too.

Chapter 5 Power Moves

1. Change your mindset and start to think about just about everything as negotiable. You'll be amazed at

what's possible. Babcock suggests starting small, and practicing. Ask the cleaners to have your clothes ready a day earlier, ask if there's a fresher cut of fish at the market, ask for an even lower rate at the hotel and an even later check-out.

2. Become a master negotiator. Set a goal for yourself to become an expert (or at least proficient) on negotiations. Take a class. Read up on negotiation skills and practice, practice, practice.

3. Share the research and results with your daughters and colleagues. Mentor young women on how to ask and negotiate.

4. Watch how you're responding to your kids when they ask for things

(I know I am!) and congratulate and encourage the girls in your life when you see them asking.

5. ASK ASK ASK! Ask for a raise, negotiate contracts, and don't discount your pricing. Sounds simple, but one of the key reasons women make less is because we don't ask for more. Let's take a page from the guys on this one, shall we?

Conclusion:

Pulling It All Together

You now know five strategies that can really accelerate things for you, and I've outlined 25 Power Moves for you to make them come alive. How are you doing? Are you taking time to complete or implement the Power Moves? You're done reading the second book, and I really want to hear about your wins! Send me an email or join in the conversation on my blog:

Mo@moxieexchange.com

www.moxieexchange.com/blog

The results you get from this book are only going to be as good as the action you take and the ideas you choose to execute on. Take ACTION. In the next book, *5 Beliefs of Winning*

Women, I share 5 beliefs that really successful women hold, most of which will surprise you. Keep working your way through the *Rock Your Moxie: Power Moves for Women Leading the Way* series and don't forget to check in with me along the way. I'd also love for you to be a part of the Rock Your Moxie: A Monthly Shot of Leadership & Success community (visit www.moxieexchange.com for more information and to register) where I lead a monthly online workshop covering the ideas and Power Moves from the books. There's no cost to attend the workshop (remember that part about needing YOU at the table?) and it will really make the content come to life for you. Plus, you're bound to connect with some very interesting and successful women who are getting after it like you.

Go, Girl! Get out there and hit the gas on your success!

The 25 Power Moves

***

Live on the Skinny Branches
1. Pick a decision you've found yourself holding back on and playing it safe about, and create a 'worst case scenario' chart to help you move forward. At the top, write down the decision, with three columns below it. In column 1, write down the worst case scenario, in column 2, how you'll know you've gotten there/indicators you have reached the worst case, in column 3 what action you will take.
2. Host a lunch/happy hour in honor of your biggest screw up. Own, celebrate, laugh at and discuss when things didn't go as planned. Share what you learned and how the 'failure' has helped move you forward.

3. Name your fears and talk them down. "If I do x I'm afraid that y will happen."
4. Do a debrief on the things you're initially categorizing as a 'failure'. Answer these questions: What went right? What did I learn? How did I just fail forward toward success?
5. Have a fan club. Yes, a fan club. Have a few key people from your inner circle that you have set up an explicit arrangement with in advance so they understand their role. When you are feeling fearful or worried about failing, call them up or meet with them to say, "This is scaring the crap out of me!" or, "I'm about to go really, really big on this one." Their job is to tell you that you are a brilliant rock star, you've got this, and that they are holding the safety net for you. They are not there to go through contingency plans, or cost benefit analysis. They are there to push

your butt out on the skinny branch and cheer you on. Trust me, it works.

Suck It Up and Shake It Off

1. Take all your gripes, complaints, slights, bad blood, excuses, health issues etc and write them on individual slips of paper. Really purge. Get it all out. Place them in a fireplace or fireproof container (old coffee cans work great), light a match, drop it in, burn the hell out of them and ceremonially LET THEM GO. I've done this with everyone from highly successful executives to teenagers and every time it's pure magic.

2. Tune in to the conversations you are a part of. You're going to be amazed how much victim talk surrounds you. Make a vow to not chime in when excuses, blame or complaints come up. Either change the conversation or walk away.

3. When you feel the urge to throw a pity party bubbling up, ask yourself these three questions: "This is hard compared to *what*?" "Is anyone going to die?" "What am I supposed to learn from this?"
4. When you find yourself replaying a failure, literally tell yourself, "Stop! We've moved on from that." Refocus by rewriting a goal you are working on. Determine two clear action items, that you can complete by the end of the day, toward accomplishing that goal.
5. Create visual prompts or mental cues to remind yourself to suck it up and shake it off. Photos, screen savers, and vivid memories that you can draw up quickly all work well.

Pay To Play

1. Add a 'learning and growth' line to your budget. You should be spending at least as

much annually on your professional and leadership learning and development as you are on your 'external' brand (clothes, shoes, hair, makeup, jewelry.) The money IS there. It's about making the choice on where you're going to spend it.

2. Subscribe to a few good magazines or blogs that are focused on leadership and success. You'll learn from their content and also find out about good programs and resources by what they are covering.
3. Poll successful women in your life about places they go for learning and growth. Ask them what organizations, programs and resources have contributed to their growth and success.
4. Commit 30 minutes a day to learning. Block it in your calendar.
5. Start a learning library. Start building up books, audios etc that have been recommended to you as growth building blocks.

Get Your Happy On

1. Wake up every day and choose happiness and joy. If you get off track, remember that you can choose again. Create joy in your world.
2. Pick one thing to keep with you that is guaranteed to make you smile. I used to carry a small picture of my husband's high school graduation photo with me (he was wearing a blue velvet tux) and would pull it out when I needed a lift.
3. Get really interested in other people and tuned in to their emotions, especially the people closest to you. Figure out the things that you do consistently and authentically that make you and other people feel good. Do more of them.
4. Choose your news media carefully. Sensationalism and fear sell, so that's what the news is loaded with. Watching it

has a big impact on your well- being. Consider skimming only headlines from a few different sources.

5. Build some silliness into your life. For example, on Friday mornings I hold what is know in our household as 'Friday morning dance party.' I turn on bad 80's music and shake my bootie all around the kitchen. My teenagers, who are wiped out by that point of the week truly *cannot* stop themselves from laughing and I feel great, too.

Ask Until Your Knees Shake

1. Change your mindset and start to think about just about everything as negotiable. You'll be amazed at what's possible. Babcock suggests starting small, and practicing. Ask the cleaners to have your clothes ready a day earlier, ask if there's a

fresher cut of fish at the market, ask for an even lower rate at the hotel and an even later check-out.
2. Become a master negotiator. Set a goal for yourself to become an expert (or at least proficient) on negotiations. Take a class. Read up on negotiation skills and practice, practice, practice.
3. Share the research and results with your daughters and colleagues. Mentor young women on how to ask and negotiate.
4. Watch how you're responding to your kids when they ask for things (I know I am!) and congratulate and encourage the girls in your life when you see them asking.
5. ASK ASK ASK! Ask for a raise, negotiate contracts, and don't discount your pricing. Sounds simple, but one of the key reasons

women make less is because we don't ask for more. Let's take a page from the guys on this one, shall we?

Author Biography

Maureen Berkner Boyt is the Founder of The Moxie Exchange Movement and its girl's leadership development program, The Go Girl Project. She is a thought partner to organizations and women serious about leadership development and learning. She holds a M.Ed. in Organizational Development, is a graduate of Corporate Coach U, and is a life-long student of leadership, business and success. She has coached over 100 leaders, founded multiple successful businesses, lived and worked internationally, and loves taking business ideas and making them come to life.

Maureen knows that every woman is capable of being an extraordinary leader and of achieving ridiculous levels of success in their lives. Her passion is bringing out the potential in female leaders and she truly believes that when women are fully represented at the executive levels in business, we will begin to solve large global problems in a meaningful way. Maureen also believes that we need to tuck the next generation of female leaders under our wings when they are still girls so that they can step into their leadership at an earlier age.

She'd love to connect with you on her blog www.moxieexchange.com/blog, by email mo@moxieexchange.com, as a part of the Rock Your Moxie: A Monthly Shot of Leadership & Success community (visit www.moxieexchange.com for more information and to register) or on LinkedIn where she can cryptically be found by typing in her name.

Made in the USA
Middletown, DE
04 February 2016